THIS IS WHO I AM

31 Truths to Meditate, Pray, & Declare

Sarah Elson

This Is Who I Am
© 2023 Sarah Elson
www.WiredForFreedom.life

Published with help from 100X Publishing:
www.100xpublishing.com

All rights reserved. No part of this publication may be reproduced, stored in a retrieval system, or transmitted in any form or by any means--for example, electronic, photocopy, recording--without the prior written permission of the publisher.

Holy Bible, New Living Translation, copyright © 1996, 2004, 2015 by Tyndale House Foundation. Used by permission of Tyndale House Publishers, Inc., Carol Stream, Illinois 60188. All rights reserved.

Scripture quotations marked TPT are from The Passion Translation®. Copyright © 2017, 2018, 2020 by Passion & Fire Ministries, Inc. Used by permission. All rights reserved. ThePassionTranslation.com.

Print ISBN: 979-8-9894830-0-6

Table of Contents

PART ONE
My Story 9

Quiet-Time Journey 10

From Me to You 15

Meditate, Renew, Transform 18

My Heart for You 29

How to Use 32

My Prayer for You 34

PART TWO: 31 "I AM" TRUTHS
1) John 1:12 37

    I AM ADOPTED INTO GOD'S FAMILY!

2) Ephesians 2:5 39

    I AM SAVED BY GRACE!

3) Genesis 1:27 41

    I AM CREATED IN THE IMAGE OF GOD!

4) 1 John 1:9 43

    I AM FORGIVEN!

5) Colossians 2:9-10 45

    I AM COMPLETE THROUGH CHRIST!

I dedicate this devotional book to my Lord, Savior, Father, King, and Lover of my soul, Jesus.

6) Romans 6:6 47

> I AM NOT A SLAVE TO SIN, IT HAS NO POWER OVER ME!

7) Jeremiah 1:5 49

> I AM SET APART & APPOINTED AS A VOICE FOR GOD ON THIS EARTH!

8) 1 Corinthians 6:19-20 51

> I AM THE TEMPLE OF THE HOLY SPIRIT. I BELONG TO HIM & I WAS BOUGHT WITH A HIGH PRICE!

9) 1 John 3:1 53

> I AM CALLED A CHILD OF GOD & HE LOVES ME VERY MUCH!

10) Colossians 3:1-3 55

> I AM HIDDEN WITH CHRIST & HAVE BEEN RAISED TO NEW LIFE WITH HIM!

11) Isaiah 49:1-3 57

> I AM CALLED BY GOD. I AM HIDDEN IN HIS HAND & I AM A SHARP ARROW IN HIS QUIVER. I WILL BRING HIM GLORY!

12) 1 Peter 2:24 59

> I AM DEAD TO SIN & I AM HEALED BECAUSE OF THE BLOOD OF JESUS!

13) Romans 8:38-39 61

> I AM LOVED BY GOD & NOTHING CAN SEPARATE ME FROM HIS LOVE!

14) John 15:5 63

> I AM A BRANCH & HE IS THE VINE, IN HIM I WILL PRODUCE MUCH FRUIT!

15) Psalm 18:32 65

> I AM ARMED WITH GOD'S STRENGTH & HE MAKES MY WAY PERFECT!

16) Isaiah 43:1-4 67

> I AM PRECIOUS TO GOD. HE IS ALWAYS WITH ME & I AM HONORED & LOVED BY HIM!

17) Zephaniah 3:17 69

> I AM GOD'S DELIGHT. HE CALMS ALL MY FEARS & HE REJOICES OVER ME WITH JOYFUL SONGS!

18) 2 Corinthians 5:17 71

> I AM A NEW CREATION IN CHRIST!

19) Isaiah 42:6-7 73

> I AM A LIGHT TO GUIDE NATIONS. I AM A LIBERATOR OF CAPTIVES!

20) 2 Timothy 1:7 75

> I AM FEARLESS & HAVE A SPIRIT OF POWER, LOVE, & A SOUND MIND!

21) John 3:16 77

> I AM A BELIEVER & HAVE ETERNAL LIFE IN JESUS!

22) Ephesians 2:10 79

> I AM GOD'S MASTERPIECE CREATED ANEW IN CHRIST JESUS TO DO GOOD THINGS!

23) Romans 8:16-17 81

> I AM AN HEIR OF GOD'S GLORY!

24) John 15:15 83

> I AM A FRIEND OF JESUS!

25) Galatians 3:27-28 85

> I AM ONE WITH CHRIST JESUS!

26) Psalm 139:14 87

> I AM A MARVELOUS, WONDERFULLY COMPLEX WORKMANSHIP OF GOD!

27) 1 Peter 2:9 89

> I AM CHOSEN, ROYAL, HOLY, & I AM A LIGHT IN THE DARKNESS!

28) 1 John 4:17 91

> I AM CONFIDENT & LIVE LIKE JESUS IN THIS WORLD!

29) 1 Corinthians 6:20 93

> I AM HIGHLY VALUED BECAUSE OF THE BLOOD OF JESUS!

30) Philippians 4:13 95

> I AM STRONG IN CHRIST JESUS & CAN DO ALL THINGS THROUGH HIS STRENGTH!

31) Song of Songs 4:7 97

> I AM BEAUTIFUL TO GOD IN EVERY WAY!

Full Declaration 98

About the Author 100

Part One

MY STORY

For over 13 years, I battled suicide ideation, self-harm, depression, fear, anxiety, and self-hatred. While I grew up in a Christian home, I didn't truly know the goodness of the Father and His radical, unconditional love for me. People ask me all the time how I got free from all the darkness to become the mighty woman of God I am today. My answer is simple: spending time with Jesus, meditating on His Word, renewing my mind with Scripture, and allowing the Holy Spirit to transform my heart.

I replaced the lies I believed about God and about myself with the truth of what God's Word says. This is how I went from a worrier to a worshiper. From fearful to fearless. From depression to full of joy. From wanting to take my life to living my life for Jesus. From self-hatred to being confident and embracing what my Maker says about me, regardless of whether I "felt it" or not. God's truth is THE truth and I live by it. As I always say, *a transformed mind leads to a transformed life*, and that is my story.

MY QUIET-TIME JOURNEY

I wanted to share with you how I journeyed through my quiet time. If you don't know where to start, I pray this will help guide you. If you are looking for some ideas on how to go deeper, I pray this will enrich your time with Jesus. The most important thing to remember is to allow the Holy Spirit to lead you in your dance together. He desires to speak to you and for you to know His voice. Trust that He will lead you. And how do you know He will? Because He says in John 16:13 that He will lead you into ALL truth.

So, here's what I did…

First, I journaled. I wrote down praises, thoughts, prayers, and anything I wanted/needed to tell the Lord. I always started with worshiping and praising Him—writing out who He is. Psalm 100:4 says to "Enter his gates with thanksgiving and his courts with PRAISE" (emphasis mine). That's the key!

My journal entries are addressed to Him; it's one of the ways I talk to Him. I did this first because then I could easily identify when He was speaking to me through my devotional and scripture.

One time I was journaling and telling the Father how overwhelmed I was about my to-do list and expressed all the things on it. Then, I opened the devotional I was reading at the time, and I kid you not, the entry started with, "a successful day isn't based on what you get done on your to-do list…" My mouth dropped! This is just one of my many experiences like this. It happens quite often. I journaled something and then my devotional spoke right to the things I just wrote about. Or when I opened my Bible, the verse was exactly the answer I needed based on what I had just written.

You don't have to journal first during your quiet time, but that's what I did. Try it out though! You will have what I like to call "you can't make this up" moments—meaning, there's no denying the Holy Spirit just answered you! Those are the best.

Second, I read my devotional. Eventually, I stopped using a devotional once I got more comfortable just going straight to the Bible. That's the purpose behind THIS devotional—getting you comfortable with going straight to the Bible. When you get to Part Two, you'll notice it won't have any of my own thoughts anymore. Why? Because I want to help you just go straight to the Word!

Third, and MOST important, I opened my Bible. I looked up the scriptures mentioned in my devotional and wrote them out in my journal. Then, I would start from the beginning of the chapter where the verse was and kept reading. Sometimes I would read the previous chapters or the chapters after too. I just did whatever I felt I was being guided to do. The Holy Spirit will lead you; I promise. Trust Him!

As I read, I highlighted or underlined any verses that I felt the Holy Spirit was speaking to me and wrote them in my journal. When specific words stood out to me, I looked up the original meaning in Hebrew or Greek using the Strong's Concordance app or Google. Doing this opens up the verse in a new and beautiful way. Did you know the Word of God is alive? Yes, and there are so many hidden treasures within it that the Holy Spirit wants to reveal to you. You may have read a verse many times before, then suddenly, a new revelation hits you and you see it in a new way. I love it when this happens!

So, I would journal alongside my reading and note anything the Lord was showing me. Finally, I went back to the verses I wrote down and declared them out loud to finish my quiet time. As I went about my day, I reflected on what He said to me earlier and talked to

Jesus about it. I would think on the verse and speak out what I remembered. This is what meditating is all about, which I will get to in just a bit.

Be encouraged—this doesn't have to take hours. It can take as long as you have. Don't feel obligated to make your quiet time look like mine or anyone else's. This is YOUR relationship with Jesus. I simply wanted to share with you what I have done because I've seen how it's helped others. The most important part of all of this is opening your Bible every day and meditating on God's Word, even if it's ONE verse. That ONE verse is more than just words; it's supernatural and can transform you from the inside out when you truly believe it.

Spending time with Jesus, talking to Him, and allowing Him to speak to me through His Word and meditating on it is what changed my whole life. As I began to memorize scriptures one by one, I used God's truth to destroy the lies and replace them with His Word. My mind and life have been and continue to be transformed by God's Word and His presence. I am confident as you spend time with Him, the same will happen for you, my friend.

FROM ME TO YOU

Let me tell you why I created this for you. When I was first starting out in my journey of really connecting with Jesus and having quiet time, I didn't know where to start. I felt overwhelmed and intimidated. But I knew Jesus said to come like a little child (Matthew 18:2-5). So, that's what I did. I kept it simple.

For me, using a devotional was helpful for a starting point. However, I didn't want to just open that and never open my Bible. I needed to get the Word of God in my heart and memorize it so that I would believe it. As I mentioned before, my hope is to lead you straight into opening the Bible for yourself. In Part Two, each day has one scripture for you to meditate on, pray out loud, and declare out loud who you are. As you dive into your Bible, I know the Holy Spirit will take you on a beautiful journey, transforming you daily if you allow Him to.

Whenever I started my quiet time, I always had these things nearby: My Bible, my journal, a devotional, a cup of coffee, and some instrumental worship playing. The cup of coffee is where the idea for this devotional guide came from. I always knew one day I wanted to design a coffee cup. When that time came, the Lord showed me a vision of the design. It had 31 verses that spoke to our identity in Christ and then a power statement: "THIS IS WHO I AM." I saw it being more than just a cup; but multifunctional! I LOVE multifunctional things, don't you? This cup is a simple, practical, and powerful tool to use in your quiet time with Jesus.

P.S. You can use this devotional without the cup, of course.

Here's the vision I saw: You grab your "THIS IS WHO I AM" cup and pour in your favorite drink. You found a comfy spot to sit and have your special time with Jesus. Each day, you picked a verse, turned to it and started to read. Then, I saw Jesus take the lead, and the two of you went on a beautiful journey in His Word together. At the end of your quiet time, I saw you becoming more confident in who He says you are. You closed your Bible and declared out loud, "THIS IS WHO I AM!"

You can use this guide in the same way. Open this book up to the table of contents, and read whatever statement or verse stands out. You can go in order or open to a random page and believe by faith that's what the Lord wants you to meditate on! You can turn it into a 31-week thing, meditating on the same verse/passage for a week, or meditate on the same verse/passage for a whole month. There are no rules, it's up to you! Just enjoy your time with Jesus and let Him fill your cup!

If you have the mug, yay I'm so glad! But if you don't and you're thinking, "But Sarah, I need this cup you keep talking about!" I got you covered. Just scan the QR code below and it will take you right to it!

MEDITATE > RENEW > TRANSFORM

Your thoughts and beliefs are either rooted in truth or rooted in lies. Truth comes from God and His Word. Lies come from Satan, the enemy. Did you know that whatever you believe you give power to? When you believe what the enemy tells you, you give him power in your life. When you believe what God says about you, you give Him power in your life. Your mind and heart should be like a tree of life and truth. Unfortunately, most of us have some beliefs that may feel true, but the root is actually a lie.

Ultimately, we want every root of every thought in our

hearts and minds to come from God's truth. This is a process, and it's done through a relationship with Jesus and spending time with Him. This book will help you get into His Word and spend time with Jesus, the lover of your soul and the only one who can transform you.

Before I tell you how to practically use this devotional, I want to tell you the meaning of three important words: Meditate. Renew. Transform.

MEDITATE

What do you think of when you hear the word *meditate*? Do you think of sitting in silence? Do you think of emptying your mind? Do you think of just letting your thoughts pass by in a non-judgmental way? If you do, it's understandable; that's what is being taught in the world for the most part, especially with the influence of Eastern religions and New-Age practices. In Eastern religions, meditation can be sitting in silence. It can be emptying your mind and training yourself to think about nothing or focus on a mantra. Or it can be sitting silently and letting thoughts pass by like something floating down a river—good, bad, or indifferent, thoughts just pass on by.

Did you know this is exactly the *opposite* of what "meditate" means in the Bible? Biblical meditation is thinking about God's Word in your mind *and* is also about using your VOICE! It's speaking God's Word out loud. Why is it important to speak the Word of God out loud? When God created the world, He spoke it into existence. We were created in His image and after His likeness. So, in the same way, our words create worlds.

Another thing—did you know you aren't supposed to just let bad thoughts pass by? You are supposed to take them captive. What does that mean? It means every thought that comes your way needs to line up with what Scripture says. Think of Scripture as a spear; you use that spear and interrogate the thought. You don't just give it access to your mind. If it doesn't line up with what Scripture says, you cast it down and deny it access! I will explain this more in the "Renew" section.

I discovered I had been meditating on God's Word this way before I even knew that's what the word means. One day, I was sitting in my car, talking to the Lord about meditation and how it's not about emptying my mind but filling it with His Word. As I fill my thoughts with His Word, the lies are driven out. Then, I heard in my spirit Joshua 1:8, which says, "Study this Book of Instruction continually. Meditate on it day and night so you will be sure to obey everything written in it. Only then will you prosper and succeed in all you do." The Holy Spirit told me to look up the original Hebrew of the word *meditate* in the verse (using the Strong's Concordance). It blew my mind. Here's what it means!

In the original Hebrew, *meditate* in this verse is:

"hagah'" (pronounced "daw-gaw")- to murmur (in pleasure or anger); by implication, to ponder: imagine, meditate, mourn, mutter, roar, speak, study, talk, utter.

MURMUR. MUTTER. SPEAK. TALK. UTTER. And my favorite…ROAR!

This is why I encourage you to not only read the Word but speak it out! When you speak it out, your spirit hears it. Not only that, but you are speaking the Word of God into your atmosphere, and the Word of God shifts atmospheres! It also means to ponder and imagine, so that's the "thinking on" aspect of meditating. It's like chewing on it and savoring it. Biblical meditation is both confession and reflection!

Let me practically break this down to you over the next few sections and make it simple. Say you're like I was, and you struggle with worry. I will use "worry" as our example and guide you through how to meditate, renew, and transform your mind.

What can you do to overcome this lie? Start by looking up scriptures that speak to not being in fear, not worrying, and trusting God. The Word of God has a lot to say about worry! Meditate on those verses. You can write them down and put them in places you will see every day. Memorize them and speak them out loud over yourself. Pray these verses out and make them into personal declarations.

By reflecting on and confessing these truths, you are meditating on God's Word. Meditation is followed by your mind being RENEWED!

RENEW

Romans 12:2 (The Passion Translation):
"Stop imitating the ideals and opinions of the culture around you, but be inwardly transformed by the Holy Spirit through a total reformation of how you think. This will empower you to discern God's will as you live a beautiful life, satisfying and perfect in his eyes."

The word *renew* is the word *reformation* in The Passion Translation. The definition in the Strong's

Concordance for the original Greek word is:

"Anakaínōsis"-renovation, a complete change.

It's like renovating a house—out with the old, in with the new. You change things around. You update things. This is a simple way to understand it. When you're meditating on God's Word, it enters your thoughts. At some point, the lies that have been there will be confronted by what God says and the lies are kicked out by you partnering with the truth! You're updating your thinking, and the old negative patterns and ugly thoughts aren't serving you anymore; it's time to upgrade! The lies must go!

Did you know that you don't have to entertain every thought that comes your way? Not every thought that enters your mind is your own thought. Remember, you have an enemy who wants to destroy you by getting you to believe his lies rather than God's truth. So, renewing your mind is how you shut the liar down.

Let's go back to the "worry" example. You start worrying about something. You know you've been a worrier for as long as you can remember. But since you've been reading and meditating on Scripture, you realize there are a lot of verses where God says *not* to worry. And you just don't want this worry thing to have a hold on you anymore. You remember Philippians 4:6-7 which says, "Don't worry about anything; instead, pray about everything. Tell God what you need, and thank him for all he has done. Then you will experience God's peace, which exceeds anything we can understand. His peace will guard your hearts and minds as you live in Christ Jesus."

So, you take the worry thought captive (that was sent by the enemy), and you say out loud, "I cast down worry right now in Jesus' name. I will not worry about anything, but I will praise You Jesus for who You are. You are with me. You will give me wisdom in this situation. You are faithful to carry me through this. Thank You, Jesus, for who You are. I thank You for Your peace right now to guard my heart and my mind."

As you keep doing this every time a worry thought comes your way, that lie will begin to lose its power and the hold it's had on you for so long. Does that make sense? The negative thought pattern starts to get disrupted by truth and will be uprooted like a weed. How? Because now you are stopping it from flourishing when it's trying to invade, and you've uprooted it and replaced it with truth. So, it has nowhere to take root in your mind and heart.

In Part Two, you will see I turned the verse into a prayer for you to declare out loud. I love to take Scripture and turn it into a prayer or declaration. I have taught a lot of people in my life to pray using Scripture. They're always amazed at how simple it is and how powerful it is. Yes, it's simple. Come like a child, remember? Simple can be powerful—never forget that!

While it's simple, I believe one of the most powerful ways to pray is to pray out God's Word! In Luke 4, when Jesus was in the desert and Satan came to tempt Him, it was the Word of God Jesus spoke out that made the devil flee. If that's what Jesus did, then that's what I'm doing too. What about you?

This leads us into being TRANSFORMED.

TRANSFORM

Romans 12:2 TPT:
"Stop imitating the ideals and opinions of the culture around you, but be inwardly transformed by the Holy Spirit through a total reformation of how you think. This will empower you to discern God's will as you live a beautiful life, satisfying and perfect in his eyes."

In the Strong's Concordance, *transform* in the original Greek is:

"Metamorphóō"- change, transfigure, transform, literally or figuratively.

When you read the Word of God and you meditate on it, through confession and reflection, you renew your mind with it, stopping lies from taking over. Then what happens? You are supernaturally changed, transfigured, and transformed. There is a total reformation/renewal of how you think. Metamorphoo is where we get the word *metamorphosis*, like what a butterfly experiences! It goes from a caterpillar to a butterfly. You come to Jesus one way, but you allow Him to transform you into a new person by changing the way you think!

Let's look at the "worry" example one more time. Since you have been meditating on what God says about worry, you have been renewing your mind. You are quick to worship instead of worry. You recognize when the enemy is whispering lies and you don't give him access anymore. What easily tripped you up before doesn't. You remain in a place of peace because you know Jesus is with you and He will give you the wisdom you need to navigate the situation or environment. You've been transformed from a worrier to a worshipper!

I hope leading you through this example helps you easily understand the process of meditating, renewing, and being transformed. When you MEDITATE on God's Word, your mind gets RENEWED, and your life TRANSFORMS!

MY HEART FOR YOU

My heart is that this would help you open your Bible each day. I trust the Holy Spirit *will* speak to you through these truths. I trust you *will* hear His voice as you spend time with Him. He is trustworthy! Every day He is waiting to share His heart with you. He wants you to know not only who He is but what He says about you. You can't be who God called you to be if you don't know what He says about you. My hope is for you to grow in your Godfidence each day and walk in who you were created to be!

I want to remind you, friend, that your quiet time with Jesus doesn't need to be complicated. You don't need to spend long hours studying to grow in your walk with the Lord. Meditating on even one powerful truth a day, praying it out, and declaring it over yourself will change your life. The key is believing it by faith. Romans 10:17 says, "So faith comes from hearing, that is, hearing the Good News about Christ." When you read the Word of God and you use your voice to pray it and declare it out loud, you hear it and it gets in your spirit. In hearing it, you begin to believe it by faith. And what you believe, you will become.

There is a spiritual battle over our identity, and as children of the Most High God, it's vital that we know our identity in Christ and walk in it. I need you to know yours, and you need me to know mine! Why? Because there's a world waiting to know who Jesus is and what He says about them! We must walk in what we believe if we want to reach those who don't know Him. If you have any beliefs about God or yourself and they don't align with what Scripture says, then those are lying thought patterns. I promise you, friend, you don't want those lies to stay in your heart and mind because they affect your life. Second Corinthians 10:3-

5 says the weapons of our warfare are not of this world, but they are mighty for pulling down strongholds. Strongholds are beliefs and thought patterns built in your thought life. They can be strongholds of truth or strongholds of lies. We use God's Word to destroy the lying thought patterns/strongholds and replace them with God's truth.

As you read the scriptures in Part Two, write them down, pray, and declare them out, you will become more confident in who God says you are. I pray this simple devotional helps you come like a child, open your Bible, and leads you into a beautiful and transforming time with the lover of your soul, King Jesus. I promise you, if you embrace what God says about you and believe it, you will never be the same! As you replace lies with truth, one by one, you will be changed. Friend, I am SO excited for you! Here's to being transformed by the renewing of your mind!

Love,
Sarah

HOW TO USE

Part Two has 31 "I AM" truths for you to read, pray, and declare as you spend time with Jesus.

Here's how to practically use this:
- Open your Bible to the verse (you can go in order or pick one that stands out).
  - Read it out (you can look up different translations).
  - Write it out (in a journal or on a note card you can write out the verse, prayer, and declaration).
  - Pray it out.
  - Declare it out.
- Go to the beginning of the chapter the verse is in and start reading.
- Highlight and write down ANY other verses that stand out or the Holy Spirit brings to your attention.
- From that place, keep reading as long as you desire. You can read the chapters after or

before—however you are led!
- While you're reading, if a word stands out to you, use a study resource like Strong's Concordance (you can buy the app or use an online resource like Bible Hub) to look up the original meaning. If it's in the Old Testament, look up the word in the original Hebrew. If it's in the New Testament, look it up in the original Greek. Doing this will give you a deeper understanding of what the word means, which gives you a deeper and richer understanding of what God is revealing to you.
- When your quiet time is coming to an end, go back to the verse:
    - Read it out.
    - Pray it out.
    - Declare it out.

MY PRAYER FOR YOU

"Heavenly Father, I thank You for my beautiful friend who desires to spend time with You and know You more. Jesus, thank You for how You've transformed my life through Your Word and Your presence. I ask that what You have done in my life, You would do in their life and even greater. Holy Spirit, breathe upon Your Word each time they open their Bible, and take them on a journey with You. I pray they would tangibly feel Your presence as they spend time with You. Holy Spirit, thank You for Your faithfulness to lead them into ALL truth. I pray that the eyes of their understanding will be opened and their hearts be flooded with Your light. I pray that any lies about You or themselves would be exposed. I declare Your Word of truth would overpower the lies and destroy them. I thank You that as they meditate on Your truth and declare it out loud, their minds would be renewed and their life transformed. I thank You for Your faithfulness to reveal to them who they are. I pray all of this in Your precious and holy name, Jesus. Amen."

Part Two

31 TRUTHS

READ

PRAY

DECLARE

I AM ADOPTED INTO GOD'S FAMILY!

john 1:12

READ IT OUT:
"But to all who believed him and accepted him, he gave the right to become children of God."
John 1:12

PRAY IT OUT:
"Father, I thank You for giving me the right to become Your child because I believe You and accept You as my Lord and Savior."

DECLARE IT OUT:
"I am adopted into God's family, and I am a child of God. This is who I am!"

I AM SAVED BY GRACE!

ephesians 2:5

READ IT OUT:

"...that even though we were dead because of our sins, he gave us life when he raised Christ from the dead. It is only by God's grace that you have been saved!"

Ephesians 2:5

PRAY IT OUT:

"Lord, I thank You for saving me by Your grace. Even though I was dead because of my sins, I praise You for giving me life when You raised Christ from the dead."

DECLARE IT OUT:

"I am saved by grace. This is who I am!"

I AM CREATED IN THE IMAGE OF GOD!

genesis 1:27

READ IT OUT:
"So God created human beings in his own image. In the image of God he created them; male and female he created them."
Genesis 1:27

PRAY IT OUT:
"God, I thank You and praise You for creating me in Your image."

DECLARE IT OUT:
"I am created in the image of God. This is who I am!"

I AM FORGIVEN & CLEANSED FROM ALL WICKEDNESS!

1 john 1:9

READ IT OUT:
"But if we confess our sins to him, he is faithful and just to forgive us our sins and to cleanse us from all wickedness."

1 John 1:9

PRAY IT OUT:
"Lord, I thank You that You are faithful and just to forgive me of my sins and cleanse me from all wickedness when I confess my sins to You."

DECLARE IT OUT:
"I am forgiven and cleansed from all wickedness. This is who I am!"

I AM COMPLETE THROUGH MY UNION WITH CHRIST!

colossians 2:9-10

READ IT OUT:
"For in Christ lives all the fullness of God in a human body. So you are also complete through your union with Christ, who is the head over every ruler and authority."
Colossians 2:9-10

PRAY IT OUT:
"Jesus, I thank You that I am complete in my union with You. You are the head over every ruler and authority, and in You lies all the fullness of God in a human body."

DECLARE IT OUT:
"I am complete through my union with Christ. This is who I am!"

I AM NOT A SLAVE TO SIN. IT HAS NO POWER OVER ME!

romans 6:6

READ IT OUT:
"We know that our old sinful selves were crucified with Christ so that sin might lose its power in our lives. We are no longer slaves to sin."

Romans 6:6

PRAY IT OUT:
"I praise You, Jesus, that my old sinful self was crucified with You so that sin loses its power in my life. I thank You that I am no longer a slave to sin."

DECLARE IT OUT:
"I am not a slave to sin. It has no power over me. This is who I am!"

I AM SET APART & APPOINTED AS A VOICE FOR GOD ON THIS EARTH!

jeremiah 1:5

READ IT OUT:
"I knew you before I formed you in your mother's womb. Before you were born I set you apart and appointed you as my prophet to the nations."

Jeremiah 1:5

PRAY IT OUT:
"Lord, I thank You for knowing me before You formed me in my mother's womb. I praise You for setting me apart and appointing me as a voice on the earth."

DECLARE IT OUT:
"I am set apart and appointed as a voice for God on this earth. This is who I am!"

I AM THE TEMPLE OF THE HOLY SPIRIT. I BELONG TO HIM & I WAS BOUGHT WITH A HIGH PRICE!

1 corinthians 6:19-20

READ IT OUT:
"Don't you realize that your body is the temple of the Holy Spirit, who lives in you and was given to you by God? You do not belong to yourself, for God bought you with a high price. So you must honor God with your body."
1 Corinthians 6:19-20

PRAY IT OUT:
"Thank You, Jesus, that my body was given to me by God and it is a temple of the Holy Spirit and You live in me. I do not belong to myself but to You, God. I will honor You, Lord, with my body because You bought me with a high price."

DECLARE IT OUT:
"I am the temple of the Holy Spirit. I belong to Him and I was bought with a high price.
This is who I am!"

I AM CALLED A CHILD OF GOD. HE LOVES ME VERY MUCH!

1 john 3:1

READ IT OUT:
"See how very much our Father loves us, for he calls us his children, and that is what we are! But the people who belong to this world don't recognize that we are God's children because they don't know him."
1 John 3:1

PRAY IT OUT:
"Father, I thank You that You love me so much and You call me Your child! I pray that people will know You, Jesus."

DECLARE IT OUT:
"I am called a child of God. He loves me very much. This is who I am!"

I AM HIDDEN WITH CHRIST & I HAVE BEEN RAISED TO NEW LIFE WITH HIM!

colossians 3:1-3

READ IT OUT:
"Since you have been raised to new life with Christ, set your sights on the realities of heaven, where Christ sits in the place of honor at God's right hand. Think about things of heaven, not the things of earth. For you died to this life, and your real life is hidden with Christ in God."
Colossians 3:1-3

PRAY IT OUT:
"I praise You, Lord, for I have been raised to new life with You. I will set my sights on the realities of heaven, where You sit in the place of honor at God's right hand. I will think about things of heaven and not of the earth. I thank You that I am dead to this life and my real life is hidden with You, Christ, in God."

DECLARE IT OUT:
"I am hidden with Christ, and I have been raised to new life with Him. This is who I am!"

I AM CALLED BY GOD. I AM HIDDEN IN HIS HAND & I AM A SHARP ARROW IN HIS QUIVER. I WILL BRING HIM GLORY!

isaiah 49:1-3

READ IT OUT:
"Listen to me, all you in distant lands! Pay attention, you who are far away! The Lord called me before my birth; from within the womb he called me by name. He made my words of judgment as sharp as a sword. He has hidden me in the shadow of his hand. I am like a sharp arrow in his quiver. He said to me, 'You are my servant, Israel, and you will bring me glory.'"
Isaiah 49:1-3

PRAY IT OUT:
"I praise You, Father, for calling me before my birth and calling me by name in my mother's womb.
I thank You that I'm hidden in the shadow of Your hand. You say I am a sharp arrow in Your quiver and I will bring You glory."

DECLARE IT OUT:
"I am called by God. I am hidden in His hand and I am a sharp arrow in His quiver. I will bring Him glory. This is who I am!"

I AM DEAD TO SIN & I AM HEALED BECAUSE OF THE BLOOD OF JESUS!

1 peter 2:24

READ IT OUT:
"He personally carried our sins in his body on the cross so that we can be dead to sin and live for what is right. By his wounds you are healed."
1 Peter 2:24

PRAY IT OUT:
"Jesus, I thank You and praise You because You carried my sins in Your body on the cross. You did this so I would be dead to sin and live for what is right. I thank You that by Your wounds, I am healed."

DECLARE IT OUT:
"I am dead to sin and I am healed because of the blood of Jesus. This is who I am!"

I AM LOVED BY GOD. NOTHING CAN SEPARATE ME FROM HIS LOVE!

romans 8:38-39

READ IT OUT:
"And I am convinced that nothing can ever separate us from God's love. Neither death nor life, neither angels nor demons, neither our fears for today nor our worries about tomorrow- not even the powers of hell can separate us from God's love. No power in the sky above or in the earth below- indeed, nothing in all creation will ever be able to separate us from the love of God that is revealed in Christ Jesus our Lord."
Romans 8:38-39

PRAY IT OUT:
"Lord God, I thank You that nothing can ever separate me from Your love. Death nor life, angels nor demons, nor fears and worries, not even the powers of hell can separate me from Your love. There is no power in the sky above or in the earth below. There is nothing in all of creation that will ever separate me from Your love that is revealed in Christ Jesus my Lord."

DECLARE IT OUT:
"I am loved by God. Nothing can separate me from His love. This is who I am!"

I AM A BRANCH & HE IS THE VINE; IN HIM I WILL PRODUCE MUCH FRUIT!

john 15:5

READ IT OUT:
"Yes, I am the vine; you are the branches. Those who remain in me, and I in them, will produce much fruit. For apart from me you can do nothing."

John 15:5

PRAY IT OUT:
"Jesus, You are the vine and I am Your branch. I thank You that Your Word says when I remain in You and You remain in me, You will produce much fruit in my life. I know that apart from You I can do nothing."

DECLARE IT OUT:
"I am a branch and He is the vine; in Him I will produce much fruit. This is who I am!"

I AM ARMED WITH GOD'S STRENGTH. HE MAKES MY WAY PERFECT!

psalm 18:32

READ IT OUT:
"God arms me with strength, and he makes my way perfect."
Psalm 18:32

PRAY IT OUT:
"Lord, I thank You for arming me with strength and making my way perfect."

DECLARE IT OUT:
"I am armed with God's strength. He makes my way perfect. This is who I am!"

I AM PRECIOUS TO GOD. HE IS ALWAYS WITH ME. I AM HONORED & LOVED BY HIM!

isaiah 43:1-4

READ IT OUT:

"But now, O Jacob, listen to the Lord who created you. O Israel, the one who formed you says, 'Do not be afraid, for I have ransomed you. I have called you by name; you are mine. When you go through deep waters, I will be with you. When you go through rivers of difficulty, you will not drown. When you walk through the fire of oppression, you will not be burned up; the flames will not consume you. For I am the Lord, your God, the Holy One of Israel, your Savior. I gave Egypt as a ransom for your freedom; I gave Ethiopia and Seba in your place. Others were given in exchange for you. I traded their lives for yours because you are precious to me. You are honored, and I love you.'" Isaiah 43:1-4

PRAY IT OUT:

"Lord, thank You for creating me and forming me. I will not be afraid because You have ransomed me. You call me by name and I am Yours. You are with me when I go through deep waters. I will never drown through rivers of difficulty. Even when I go through the fire of oppression, I will not be burned up or consumed by the flames. I praise You because You are my Lord and my Savior. You say I am precious to You and I am honored. Thank You for loving me."

DECLARE IT OUT:

"I am precious to God. He is always with me. I am honored and loved by Him. This is who I am!"

I AM GOD'S DELIGHT. HE CALMS ALL MY FEARS & REJOICES OVER ME WITH JOYFUL SONGS!

zephaniah 3:17

READ IT OUT:
"For the Lord your God is living among you. He is a mighty savior. He will take delight in you with gladness. With his love, he will calm all your fears. He will rejoice over you with joyful songs."
Zephaniah 3:17

PRAY IT OUT:
"God, You are my mighty Savior and You live in me. I thank You for delighting in me with gladness. I praise You for calming all my fears with Your love. I thank You for rejoicing over me with joyful songs."

DECLARE IT OUT:
"I am God's delight. He calms all my fears and rejoices over me with joyful songs. This is who I am!"

I AM A NEW CREATION IN CHRIST!

2 corinthians 5:17

READ IT OUT:
"This means that anyone who belongs to Christ has become a new person. The old life is gone; a new life has begun!"
2 Corinthians 5:17

PRAY IT OUT:
"I praise You, Jesus, because in belonging to You, I am a new creation and my old life is gone."

DECLARE IT OUT:
"I am a new creation in Christ. This is who I am!"

I AM A LIGHT TO GUIDE NATIONS & A LIBERATOR OF CAPTIVES!

isaiah 42:6-7

READ IT OUT:
"I, the Lord, have called you to demonstrate my righteousness. I will take you by the hand and guard you, and I will give you to my people, Israel, as a symbol of my covenant with them. And you will be a light to guide the nations. You will open the eyes of the blind. You will free the captives from prison, releasing those who sit in dark dungeons."
Isaiah 42:6-7

PRAY IT OUT:
"Lord, I thank You for calling me to demonstrate Your righteousness. You take me by the hand and guard me. You call me a light to guide nations. You say that I will open the eyes of the blind, free captives from prison, and I will release those who sit in dark dungeons."

DECLARE IT OUT:
"I am a light to guide nations and a liberator of captives. This is who I am!"

I AM FEARLESS & HAVE A SPIRIT OF POWER, LOVE, & A SOUND MIND!

2 Timothy 1:7

READ IT OUT:
"For God has not given us a spirit of fear and timidity, but of power, love, and self-discipline."
2 Timothy 1:7

PRAY IT OUT:
"God, I thank You for giving me a spirit of power, love, and a sound mind. You have not given me a spirit of fear or timidity."

DECLARE IT OUT:
"I am fearless and have a spirit of power, love, and a sound mind. This is who I am!"

I AM A BELIEVER & HAVE ETERNAL LIFE IN JESUS!

john 3:16

READ IT OUT:
"For this is how God loves the world: He gave his one and only Son, so that everyone who believes in him will not perish but have eternal life."
John 3:16

PRAY IT OUT:
"I praise You, God, because You gave the world Jesus, and You say that everyone who believes in Him will not perish but have eternal life.
Thank you for eternal life, Jesus."

DECLARE IT OUT:
"I am a believer and have eternal life in Jesus.
This is who I am!"

I AM GOD'S MASTERPIECE, CREATED ANEW IN CHRIST JESUS TO DO GOOD THINGS!

ephesians 2:10

READ IT OUT:
"For we are God's masterpiece. He has created us anew in Christ Jesus, so we can do the good things he planned for us long ago."
Ephesians 2:10

PRAY IT OUT:
"I praise You, Lord, for making me Your masterpiece. I thank You for creating me new in Christ Jesus so I can do the good things You planned for me long ago."

DECLARE IT OUT:
"I am God's masterpiece, created anew in Christ Jesus to do good things! This is who I am!"

I AM AN HEIR OF GOD'S GLORY!

romans 8:16-17

READ IT OUT:
"For his Spirit joins with our spirit to affirm that we are God's children. And since we are his children, we are his heirs. In fact, together with Christ we are heirs of God's glory. But if we are to share his glory, we must also share his suffering."
Romans 8:16-17

PRAY IT OUT:
"I thank You, Lord, that Your Spirit joins with my spirit and affirms I am Your child. Thank You for making me Your heir and an heir of Your glory. I know that if I am to share in Your glory, I will also share in Your suffering. Lord it's an honor to live my life for You because You gave Your life for me."

DECLARE IT OUT:
"I am an heir of God's glory. This is who I am!"

I AM
A FRIEND
OF JESUS!

john 15:15

READ IT OUT:
"I no longer call you slaves, because a master doesn't confide in his slaves. Now you are my friends, since I have told you everything the Father told me."

John 15:15

PRAY IT OUT:
"Jesus, thank You for calling me Your friend."

DECLARE IT OUT:
"I am a friend of Jesus. This is who I am!"

I AM ONE WITH CHRIST JESUS!

galatians 3:27-28

READ IT OUT:
"And all who have been united with Christ in baptism have put on Christ, like putting on new clothes. There is no longer Jew or Gentile, slave or free, male and female. For you are all one in Christ Jesus."
Galatians 3:27-28

PRAY IT OUT:
"I thank You, Lord, for giving me new clothes and making me one with Christ Jesus."

DECLARE IT OUT:
"I am one with Christ Jesus. This is who I am!"

I AM A MARVELOUS, WONDERFULLY COMPLEX WORKMANSHIP OF GOD!

psalm 139:14

READ IT OUT:
"Thank you for making me so wonderfully complex!
Your workmanship is marvelous—
how well I know it."
Psalm 139:14

PRAY IT OUT:
"God, I thank You and praise You for making me so wonderfully complex. You have made me a marvelous workmanship, and I desire to know it well."

DECLARE IT OUT:
"I am a marvelous, wonderfully complex workmanship of God. This is who I am!"

I AM CHOSEN, ROYAL, HOLY, & I AM A LIGHT IN THE DARKNESS!

1 peter 2:9

READ IT OUT:
"But you are not like that, for you are a chosen people. You are royal priests, a holy nation, God's very own possession. As a result, you can show others the goodness of God, for he called you out of the darkness into his wonderful light."
1 Peter 2:9

PRAY IT OUT:
"I thank You, Father, that I am chosen. You call me a royal priest, a holy nation, and Your very own possession. I thank You that I can show others Your goodness. I praise You for calling me out of the darkness and bringing me into Your wonderful light."

DECLARE IT OUT:
"I am chosen, royal, holy, and I am a light in the darkness. This is who I am!"

I AM CONFIDENT & LIVE LIKE JESUS IN THIS WORLD!

1 john 4:17

READ IT OUT:
"And as we live in God, our love grows more perfect. So we will not be afraid on the day of judgment, but we can face him with confidence because we live like Jesus here in this world."

1 John 4:17

PRAY IT OUT:
"Thank You, Lord, that my love grows more perfect in You. Help me to live like You, Jesus, here in this world."

DECLARE IT OUT:
"I am confident and live like Jesus in this world. This is who I am!"

I AM HIGHLY VALUED BECAUSE OF THE BLOOD OF JESUS!

1 corinthians 6:20

READ IT OUT:
"...for God bought you with a high price.
So you must honor God with your body."
1 Corinthians 6:20

PRAY IT OUT:
"God, I praise You and thank You for buying me with a high price! I will honor You with my body."

DECLARE IT OUT:
"I am highly valued because of the blood of Jesus.
This is who I am!"

I AM STRONG IN CHRIST JESUS & CAN DO ALL THINGS BY HIS STRENGTH!

philippians 4:13

READ IT OUT:
"For I can do everything through Christ,
who gives me strength."
Philippians 4:13

PRAY IT OUT:
"I thank You, Jesus, that I can do everything through You because You give me strength."

DECLARE IT OUT:
"I am strong in Christ Jesus and can do all things by His strength. This is who I am!"

I AM BEAUTIFUL TO GOD IN EVERY WAY!

songs of songs 4:7

READ IT OUT:
"You are altogether beautiful, my darling,
beautiful in every way."
Song of Songs 4:7

PRAY IT OUT:
"Lord, thank You for calling me Your darling.
You say I am altogether beautiful in every way."

DECLARE IT OUT:
"I am beautiful to God in every way.
This is who I am!"

"I AM" DECLARATION

"I am adopted into God's family! I am saved by grace! I am created in the image of God! I am forgiven and cleansed from all wickedness! I am complete through my union in Christ! I am not a slave to sin; it has no power over me! I am set apart and appointed as a voice for God on this earth! I am the temple of the Holy Spirit! I belong to Him, and I was bought with a high price! I am called a child of God, and He loves me very much! I am hidden with Christ, and I have been raised to new life with Him! I am called by God! I am hidden in His hand, and I am a sharp arrow in His quiver! I will bring Him glory! I am dead to sin, and I am healed because of the blood of Jesus! I am loved by God, and nothing can separate me from His love! I am a branch, and He is the vine; in Him I will produce much fruit! I am armed with God's strength, and He makes my way perfect! I am precious to God. He is always with me, and I'm honored and loved by Him! I am God's delight! He calms all my fears, and He rejoices over me with joyful songs! I am a new creation in Christ! I am a light to guide nations and a liberator of captives! I am fearless and have a spirit of power, love, and a sound mind! I'm a believer and have eternal life in Jesus! I am God's masterpiece, created anew in Christ Jesus to do good things! I am an heir of God's glory! I am a friend of Jesus! I am one with Christ Jesus! I am a marvelous, wonderfully complex workmanship of God! I am chosen, royal, holy, and am a light in the darkness! I am confident and live like Jesus in this world! I am highly valued because of the blood of Jesus! I am strong in Christ Jesus and can do all things by His strength! I am beautiful to God in every way! I decree and declare this is who I am, in the name of Jesus!"

About the Author

Sarah is the founder of Wired for Freedom, a lifestyle company which offers jewelry, apparel, home goods, and other resources to equip and empower people in their faith. Passionate about equipping people in their identity in Christ, Sarah is an entrepreneur, author, speaker, Kingdom influencer, and minister of the Gospel. She also hosts Freedom Nights—a faith based gathering in Southern California, and leads an online community called The Well. She calls Orange County, California, home, along with her family.

Learn more now at:

WiredForFreedom.life

Connect with Sarah!

 @wiredforfreedom

 /wiredforfreedom

 info@wiredforfreedom.life

To order your "THIS IS WHO I AM" Coffee mug, scan this code:

Shop WIRED FOR FREEDOM

www.ingramcontent.com/pod-product-compliance
Lightning Source LLC
Chambersburg PA
CBHW060205050426
42446CB00013B/3000